Encourage
29 WESTCL
WESTBROOK
MARGATE
KENT CT9 5UN

EMMA BUTLER tel: ~~0085~~
07522 477910

Mindset Makeover

Shedding Toxic Beliefs to Embrace Life's Balance and Harmony

Know Grow + Glow

The Encourage Wellbeing Club

password: rKXq1aDO
1 zero

First edition

This book was professionally typeset on Reedsy.
Find out more at reedsy.com

Contents

My Journey to Balance and Harmony

I've been thinking long and hard about how to introduce myself to you, because I have so much I could tell you about me and my life, but I've realised that could be another whole book in itself. So instead, I am going to give you a brief introduction to me, and how I ended up here, writing this book on Mindset Makeover and how and more importantly, I think it's the number one thing you can do that will transform your life.

I've lived what I would consider to be a pretty normal life, filled with ups and downs. The ups came from having the most beautiful family and childhood at home. The downs came from difficult and often damaging relationships, jobs that I was really good at, but didn't love, friends that let me down, being a mum to my beautiful son who suffered with his mental health, and spending a huge amount of time on the outside looking in at things I wanted to do, but just didn't believe I could.

And there you have it. That word. **BELIEVE**. It's popped up already! You'll soon understand why it's such an important word to notice.

So, up until I was 50, I lived what I considered to be a normal existence. Lot's of good things, sprinkled with lots of heartache, pain, and discomfort. All of which resulted in physical and mental health issues for me throughout my life.

So what changed? Well, at 50, I was in the depth of my menopause, and all my physical and mental issues became heightened. I lost my confidence, my ability to think and act clearly, my mojo, my love for life and ultimately, myself.

The defining moment came when, having spent around 6 months under the care of a gynecologist consultant, to try and get to the root of why I was so unwell, I was told "It's just your menopause. There is nothing I can do for you, so you are just going to have ride through it, until it's over." In that moment, hearing those words, I felt devastated. I had a very strong memory of my mum around the same age as I was then, struggling with life. She was always crying, mostly irritable and for me, completely disconnected. At the time, I was 13 years old, and just heading into puberty. I too was experiencing the hit of hormones that both the menopause and puberty bring, so I was moody, unhappy and lost. I believed at the time that my mum was too old to understand and too tired to care. I have 4 older sisters and they all seemed to have had a wonderful relationship with my mum, but in that moment, our relationship became damaged. ***At least that is what believed.*** That was the story I owned and the one that I carried with me for many years to come. I believed I was different to my sisters. I believed my mum just couldn't cope with me.

I remember my mum being unhappy like this for about 10 years, and our relationship overall being extremely difficult. I became an unpleasant person and began to behave differently. I changed how I treated myself and those around me. This one belief had a huge impact on my life, I see that now. But back then, I believed it was true and I felt rejected and disconnected. I recall my poor dad, always trying to be the go between, always reminding my mum and I that we loved each other and that he loved us both. Bless my beautiful dad.

Back to me in the chair with the gynecologist telling me I just "had to ride through it", and I had a huge realisation. My mum had been in exactly the same place as I was now, at the same age. She was struggling with her menopause, and she suffered it for at least 10 years. I left the hospital that day believing my life as I knew it was over. That I had to face this new version of myself for at least the next 10 years. In that moment, I felt hopeless. I was also washed with guilt, as the realisation of what had happened between me and mum hit home.

At the same time this was happening to me, my mum, now 87, had just been diagnosed with Alzheimers. Everything felt like it was crumbling around me, and I believed there was no way back.

After spending a day or so reeling from the news, **I made a decision**. At the time I made it, I believed I had no choice. Now I can see that wasn't true, I always have a choice! But I'm so grateful that that's what I believed that day because it was the catalyst for change for me.

My decision was to find a way out of the mess I was in and to find a life that felt like it belonged to me. A life where I felt balanced, happy and connected. 6 years on and I'm happy to say I've achieved that and so much more.

So, why did I choose this part of my story to tell you? Well, it's because it was the first time that I knowingly changed a belief that was holding me back into one that empowered me to achieve the life I have now. I didn't know it at the time, but changing that one belief, changed everything for me. I believed I could live a life full of balance and harmony, where previously I had not.

Changing your beliefs is the most empowering thing you can do to move your life from one of pain, discomfort, unhappiness, illness and disconnection, to one where you can find true balance and harmony in your life. And don't worry if you don't know what balance and harmony looks or feels like for you yet, that's OK. It's why you are here.

Oh, and if you still haven't quite got what I am talking about here yet. Go back and read the above again, but this time, look at how many times I mention the word *"believe"* in it. It might give you some clues.

Join me now, and let's explore the power of beliefs together. I can't wait to support you on this journey of transformation.

Emma x

With love
Emma
x

Introduction: Your Journey to a Mindset Makeover

Embark on a life-changing path to reclaim your joy and purpose

So, let's begin. First a question. Do you ever find yourself just going through the motions, spending each day, almost like you're not really there? Or living each day thinking ...

- "where did it all go wrong?"
- "What happened to me?"
- "This isn't how it was meant to be for me!"

You might feel like you're just re-living the same old patterns day after day, feeling stuck, and no matter what you try, you just don't seem to be able to change it.

Well, I've been there, living day to day with hundreds of beliefs that were doing nothing for me, completely oblivious to the negative impact they were having on my life. Thankfully, that changed for me. I found a way out of the rut I was in and it was truly life changing.

It was then that I made it my mission to help other people, just like you, get the realisation that I had. That it is completely possible to break free from a life that is painful, hard, heavy and unfulfilling, and instead create a life that's full of balance, harmony and happiness. And the best thing is, you have everything you need to begin that process of freedom right now. You don't need to buy anything and you don't need to go anywhere, because all you need to do is give your mindset a bit of a makeover.

"The only way out, is through"

Before we jump right in, I also want you to know that 6 years ago, the "mindset" thing was unknown to me. Back then, I believed life was just something that happened, with its ups and downs, and there wasn't much about it that I could control. That didn't stop me trying mind you! But now I do understand it, I can see that what I was trying to control was actually out of my control, so it just made life even harder! The good bits felt like luck, and the crap bits felt, well... crap, and I thought they were just part of how life was meant to be.

But then, wham, I hit this massive roadblock, the kind that makes you stop, pay attention and listen. The kind that makes you realise you can't just keep on keeping on like you've always done.

And don't get me wrong, I'd had my fair share of roadblocks along the way, but I had somehow, against all odds, managed to keep going. I'd managed to continue to do the things I needed to do, like show up for work, keep my home safe and warm, and, once my son Miles came along, be the best mum I could be in the circumstances. But this time it was different. *It felt different.* It was like this giant wall that literally stopped me in my tracks and I couldn't find any way through it. I found I couldn't even show up for the basics, let alone anything that needed a little more effort.

Then, to add to it, I started to really doubt myself. I had lots of old, niggling beliefs and stories coming up, telling me who I was and what I was meant for. Each little nagging thought was like a brick in this massive wall of doom, with doubts and limits gradually forming around myself.

- "It's too late for me to change"
- "I've brought this on myself"
- "This is it for me now"
- "There is no way out of this"

Do any of these sound familiar? These were my go-to lines, the continuous messages in my head in a life that felt like it was on repeat, and heading in one direction only, down!

But I want you to know something right now: the walls I mention are walls built by us. We build them thought by thought, action by action. Often we build them because we think they are keeping us safe. But that just isn't true. They may appear to be keeping us safe but in reality they're holding us back. They are stopping us from doing all the good stuff that matters —like taking chances, taking action, being authentic and making moves towards a life that we truly deserve, living the life we're only dreaming of.

So this book is all about tearing down that wall, brick by brick. It's about paying attention to the disruptive, damaging and limiting beliefs that are keeping you stuck right now, and replacing them with new empowering ones that actually lift you up and push you forward, aligning everything with what really matters to you.

And the best bit! You don't need to pack your bags or head off somewhere else to start this journey. You don't have to spend money along the way, you don't need any special skills or talent and you don't need to spend a week at a retreat. You already have all you need in your hands right now. The only thing you need to get going is an open mind and the desire for change. These 2 things will give you the motivation you need to shine a light on the areas of your mind that you've not tapped into for some time (or maybe ever!). You are going to begin to question your current beliefs, and you are going to start feeding your brain with thoughts that are all about growth, resilience, and feeling good. .

So, if you're fed up with feeling like life's just happening to you, if you're ready to take the wheel and steer things in a direction you're actually excited about, then you're in the right place. **Welcome to your Mindset Makeover.**

Now, let's get going on this adventure together. I'm excited for you, because I believe the person you discover at the end of it might just be the you you've been waiting to meet.

Chapter 1: Getting Your Head Around Mindset

Discover the power of perspective and how it shapes your reality.

<u>Mindset</u>. It gets a huge amount of attention these days. If you're into social media, it's unlikely there's a day that goes by without you seeing something about Mindset. If you go to any kind of well-being class or if you work for a company that champions well-being, then the chances are Mindset is being shouted about. It's becoming something that seems to pop up over and over again.

But what is it, really? Let me take this moment to strip it back to the basics.

Imagine your mindset as a pair of glasses. These glasses are the lens through which you view the world. They colour everything in your life — from how you think about things, how you react to life's ups and downs, and the decisions you make every day, both big and small. They are your mental lens.

Now, most of the time, your mental lens is working away silently in the background, going unnoticed. It's there, doing its job, you're not really paying any attention to it, and in some cases, you won't even know it's a thing. This part of our thinking is known as *unconscious thinking*. It's the thinking we do on autopilot and it just keeps things ticking over while we're busy getting on with life. But, **and here is the really important bit**, the moment you decide to pay attention to your mental lens, to notice what it is seeing, and how it's shaping your thoughts, your actions, your behaviour and your results, that's when you will realise you've actually got the power to adjust the lens, to take off the glasses so to speak, and put on a new pair that allows you to think, feel and act differently.

Now, I'd like you to try something.

Think back to this morning, or maybe to yesterday. Think about a decision you made without really thinking about it. Maybe you hit the snooze button a few times, or you made yourself the same breakfast you have every morning, or you made yourself a cuppa with 2 sugars. These moments, these decisions (and yes they are *unconscious* decisions), as tiny as they may seem, are your mindset at work.

Why does this matter? Well, it's not the fact that you made the same breakfast you always do, or that you pressed snooze, it's about how these decisions, now formed habits, come together to shape your days, and eventually, your life. So if what you are choosing day to day is the easy instead of the challenging, the safe way instead of taking a chance, and if every time you talk yourself out of trying something new because you've convinced yourself it's not for you, that's your mindset creating your life, thought by thought.

"Do what you've always done and you will get what you always got"

But what happens if you choose to change some of those thoughts and habits, the ones that are holding you back and keeping you stuck, for some new ones that move you towards a place that feels more vibrant, more calm and more balanced? That's what we're here for. We're not just talking about adjusting a habit here and there; we're talking about going a bit deeper, and getting to those deep rooted beliefs that have been driving your life for far too long, in the wrong direction. We are talking about adjusting the SatNav of life and heading somewhere else, to a place you've been longing to go. A place full of peace, balance, harmony, contentment and joy. And, we are talking about setting up roots when we arrive and nurturing our new space daily, so it continues to grow and blossom, as will you.

So, are you ready to roll up your sleeves and get started? To start taking those small steps, one day at a time, bit by bit, so you reshape that mental landscape of yours into something that feels a bit more... well, you.

I know there are nuggets of gold tucked away in the corners of that brilliant mind of yours, just waiting to be discovered, so let's go find them now, together.

Chapter 2: Identifying Toxic Beliefs

Learn to recognise and uproot the limiting beliefs that hold you back

Okay, so now I want us to dig a bit deeper and look at something I like to call toxic beliefs. I'm not talking about the occasional bad day where you are consumed by negative thoughts; I'm referring to beliefs; they're deeper, more ingrained and they weigh you down and keep you stuck. Beliefs like "I'm just not cut out for this," "I'll never get this right," "I not capable of that", or the classic "I'm not good enough." These beliefs are the weeds in the garden of our mind, and if we don't pay attention to them, they can swallow up the beautiful things we're trying to grow, and kill them off completely.

Now, let's take a moment for reflection. Grab a cuppa, find a quiet spot, and think: is there a toxic belief that's been a constant in your life. It may be loud and proud, or it may just be a background whisper. Identifying it might take some time, but be patient with yourself. Omce you get going, you'll probably find you have many. Some common toxic beliefs include "I don't have enough time," "I'm not clever enough," and "I wouldn't be able to do that." Once you have one, write it down. Seeing it in black and white can make it seem less scary.

Now here's a crucial point I want you to understand: these beliefs, as much as they feel a part of us, are not always the truth. In fact, most of our toxic beliefs are total lies. The other really important thing about your beliefs that i want you to know is, they belong to you! You decide if you believe it, which means, and this is the transformative part, you have the power to challenge and change them. It's a total game-changer when you realise that just because something is a deeply held belief, it doesn't make it true. Our brains are pattern-seeking, meaning they'll reinforce whatever we consistently tell ourselves. This is how so many of our toxic beliefs are formed but this also means we can reprogram these patterns whenever we choose to, with new, empowering beliefs.The impact of these toxic beliefs on our lives can be profound, often stopping us from pursuing what we truly want, keeping us playing it safe, and ultimately, holding us back.

So it's time now to stop, review your list of beliefs, and to really consider how each one has limited you. Ask yourself

- how has this belief shaped the life I now live?
- what wonderful opportunities have I missed as a result of this belief?
- who might I be today if I hadn't owned this belief?
- how might I be feeling today if I didn't believe this?
- what action might I take if this belief wasn't part of me?

This exercise can sometimes be quite emotional and challenging. But that's OK because the more you see how the belief has held you back, the more you will be inspired to change it! And change it you can.

"Action is the antidote to fear"

The next step is becoming good at recognising these toxic beliefs when they surface in your daily thoughts. This requires you to be more mindful, to stop living on autopilot and moving into a more conscious state of mind, where you observe your automatic thoughts and question whether they serve you. It's about choosing not to follow the well-trodden path of safety and familiarity and instead, building that new path, the one that takes you toward who you truly want to be. Now you have this awareness, the real work of transformation can begin.

Together we'll address these beliefs head-on, dismantling them piece by piece, and in their place, we'll plant new, empowering thoughts. This process isn't about overnight change; it's a gradual reshaping of your mental landscape to create a life that's not just comfortable, but truly fulfilling.

So, let's keep going. Together, we'll weed out the toxic beliefs that have been holding you back and sow the seeds of new, empowering beliefs that will support you in growing into your fullest potential.

Chapter Three: Bringing in the Good Stuff, Empowering Beliefs

Replace old narratives with empowering beliefs to fuel your growth

Okay, so you've spent some time thinking about some of those toxic beliefs that have made themselves comfortable in your mind. You don't have to have many; just one is all you need to start making a change, and now it's time to change the story, to flip that belief on its head. For every one of those toxic beliefs that you've identified, there is a new empowering belief waiting to take its place. An empowering belief does exactly what it says on the tin; it empowers you, it gives you permission to do more, to be more.

Let's look at the examples of some of the toxic beliefs that we had earlier and see how we can flip them to an empowering belief:

"I don't have enough time."

becomes

"I choose how I spend my time."

"I'm not clever enough."

becomes

"I am able to learn more and increase my knowledge."

.

"I wouldn't be able to do that."

becomes

"I am able to do anything if I put the time and effort into it."

It's just a simple swap!

So go and grab that piece of paper where you wrote down your toxic belief(s) earlier. Now I want you to consider how this old limiting belief can *"become"* an empowering belief, just as I've just done in the example above. Take your time and write the new empowering belief down next to the old limiting one.

Doing this is really like turning a black and white photo into colour; it changes everything. Empowering beliefs are not just feel-good phrases; they are statements of truth.

More than that, they make you realise that the belief that you were holding on to was actually a lie. These new empowering beliefs remind you of what you're truly capable of, especially when the going gets tough. And remember earlier I told you that you own your beliefs. That's the great thing about it. You get to choose which ones you keep and which ones you let go of. You are the author here. You decide what beliefs are going to guide you from this point forward.

Once you start embracing your new beliefs, change begins. For the first time perhaps, you'll be looking at the world through your shiny new glasses, and just that small change is where your big results begin.

Now I know you may be thinking, hang on. It can't be that simple. I can't just change a belief, and everything around me changes. And you're right, but **it is the first step**; the next step is nurturing these beliefs, just like you do when you nurture your garden. You know you have to water it, it needs a bit of sunshine, and sometimes you have to protect it from the cold otherwise it will die. The same applies to your beliefs. You need to spend time nurturing them. Do this and you'll get the results that you're looking for. Putting that little bit of effort in, will really pay off.

"Progress, not Perfection"

So, how do you nurture a belief? The first step is giving it room to grow. A great way of doing this is by repeating it to yourself at every opportunity, maybe when you're brushing your teeth or stood waiting for the kettle to boil. Also, you want to be reminded of it often. So, write it down on a piece of paper and stick it on the fridge, or make it your screensaver on your computer, or put it in your bag. It doesn't matter where you put it, what matters is that you do put it somewhere, as a constant reminder.

Remember earlier we talked about the brain liking patterns; we want your mind to build this new pattern with this new belief because when you do, eventually it will say, "Okay, if you say so," and it will become a fact. So, give it some attention, give it some love, and before you know it, it will have taken root.

This is where the magic starts to happen. This is where we turn those "I wish" moments into "I am" statements. It's where you will start building the foundations for a life that's not just about getting by, but about thriving, and grabbing hold of every bit of joy and possibility that's out there waiting for you.

So, before you move on to the next chapter, take the time right now to give those new empowering beliefs some room to grow. Write them down, repeat them, and start making those new patterns of thought. Let them become comfortable in your brain, in your mind, let them become part of you, one belief at a time.

Chapter Four: Baby Steps to a Big-Time Mindset Shift

Implement small impactful habits for lasting change in your mindset

So, before we move on to what those baby steps are, I want you to understand that changing your beliefs is not about giving your mind a huge one-time makeover. Not at all. It's a gradual process, the little things, the daily nudges, the small adjustments that stack up and make the difference.

So, we're going to start small but think big.

Here are what I believe are three of the best ways to get your mindset makeover moving:

Daily Affirmations

An affirmation is a great way of taking that belief and affirming it to yourself. Make this a ritual every morning.

When you wake up, before you stand up from your bed, sit on the edge of it and take a moment to affirm your belief. Declare it in your head, and if you can (without disturbing anyone) say it out loud, say it with pride.

If this feels a stretch too far, then have a journal by the side of your bed and in the morning, before you do anything else, spend a few minutes writing your affirmation in the journal. A bit like when you were told to do lines at school (oh, just me then!) just write it over and over again. It's setting you up for your day and pointing you in the direction you want to go.

Mindfulness Moments

It's time to get out of your unconscious mind and into your conscious mind. Each day, agree with yourself that you are going to have three mindful moments. These are moments when you tune into your thoughts; it's a bit like people-watching, but instead of sitting there with your coffee looking out into the world, watching people go by, you're going to look inwards and observe your own thoughts.

When you notice one of those toxic beliefs trying to make its way back in, acknowledge it and then let it go by. **Don't engage with it; it doesn't belong to you anymore**. Just let it pass. You've decided which beliefs you own now, so when one of the old ones tries to make its way back, remind it there is no room. Shift your focus to your new empowering belief and give it a gentle stroke.

Gratitude Practice

Gratitude is a wonderful practice because it helps us focus on the great things we have in our life. It's especially powerful if you do it just before you go to sleep at night. So before you close your eyes ready to drift off, take a moment and think of three things you are grateful for. They could be big things or small things; it doesn't matter. Just take a moment to acknowledge them. Notice how they make you feel.

It could be something as simple as a text message you received from a friend, or the cup of tea that was made for you, or it could be something much bigger, like the home you live in or the garden you love. Whatever it is, take a moment each night to be grateful for what you have. It's a fabulous way to go off to sleep, and it makes anything that may not have gone so well that day seem less important. It moves the mind away from worry, anxiety and lack, and towards appreciation, joy and warmth.

Affirmations, Mindfulness and Gratitude. These three new steps in your life may seem really simple, but I can't stress enough how powerful they are. The daily reminder of your new belief, the very regular moments of observing your thoughts and guiding them, and the moments of gratitude, they all add up. You may not notice it at first; it takes a bit of time to feel the shift. But before you know it, you will start to notice and more importantly feel that you are heading in a new direction.

"Growth Starts Where Comfort Ends"

So start right now. Don't put it off!.

As I said before, the only thing you need to begin this process is some determination, desire, and most importantly, the willingness to give it a try. And if you've got a toxic belief coming up right now, telling you ...

"doing these things won't make a difference"

change it into an empowering one! *Let it become*

"doing these things will lead me to the place I want to go"

And in that moment right there, you saw just how easy it is for your mind to try and stop you making change, to keep you stuck! But you also saw just how quickly you can tell it where to go!

Chapter Five: Making It Stick – Living the Makeover

Solidify your new mindset and enjoy a life filled with balance and harmony

So, by now, you will have started your mindset makeover by bringing in your day-to-day practices and focusing on your new empowering beliefs, and you're probably thinking, "What's next?" Well, in all honesty there's nothing more. Rather, it's about patience and sticking with it, even when it feels like you're not getting anywhere fast.

Think of it this way: you are building something that's meant to last—a balanced, harmonious life. It took a long time for you to build that brick wall around you, and it will take time to knock it down, brick by brick. This comes by building new habits; *thinking habits*. Start simple and stick with it. Build your daily affirmations into your routine. Put a reminder on your phone so you don't forget. Block your calendar for your mindful moments and make them part of you. Get a gratitude journal and leave it in your pocket or in the car or in your bag. And every time you notice something that's made you feel good, write it down. Then, when you go to bed at night, get your journal out and read all the things that you are grateful for.

Don't make this overwhelming. Remember, it's all about baby steps. You don't need to overhaul your whole day from the minute you get up to the minute you go to bed; just pick one or two things that feel right and start there. And remember, be kind to yourself. Some days it will feel easy. You'll notice the difference. You'll feel more at ease, harmonious, and balanced, but other days it will be hard. Those are the days where doing your practice really counts. But just know that these days are okay, because they are all part of the process.

It's on the days where it feels hard that you need to remind yourself why you started this journey. You are creating a life where you decide what happens in your world, where your mindset is your strongest asset, not something that holds you back. Every small step you take, every affirmation, every mindful moment, and every bit of gratitude are all bricks in the new foundation that you are building, leading you to a happier, more balanced, and joyful life.

"Brave Is What You Are, Not What You Feel"

So keep at it. It takes time to build something that will last, and that's exactly what you're doing. Bit by bit, day by day, you're creating a new life, not just one where you get by, but one where you thrive, where you feel authentic, and you really start to feel like you.

And that is what this makeover is all about. It's not a quick fix. It's about setting down roots for lasting change, about finding that balance and harmony in the noisiest of places, and most importantly, it's about living a life that feels as good on the inside as perhaps it may look on the outside.

So, now is the time for you to start living your makeover, to set off on that journey, and to celebrate every little victory along the way.

Conclusion: Stepping into Your Happier Self

Reflect on your journey and embrace the empowered life you've created

You've made it; we've come to the end of this journey together, but for you, it's truly the beginning. By now, you will have taken those first brave steps on that new path. You're no longer stuck on that road you've been walking for so many years; you've turned the corner and you're on a path of transformation, one that starts in your mind.

So, if there's one thing I'd love you to take away from this journey we've been on together, it's this: the real magic, the power to shift your mindset and to turn your life into something more wonderful, has been in you all along.

Each new belief brings with it a chance for you to step out of that comfort zone you've spent so many years in and into a place that's much more magical. Every time you let go of a toxic belief, you are choosing you. Every choice you make, every thought you nurture, and every empowering belief that you decide to hold close takes you one step closer to the balance and harmony that you've been missing.

"Your Mindset Is Your Greatest Asset"

So, don't rush it. ***Enjoy it***. It's not about the destination; it's about the journey. Think of it as a leisurely stroll on a new path where you get to see loads of new, exciting things along the way. Take them all in—the highs and the lows and everything in between—because each step, each stumble, and each triumph is part of your exciting new adventure.

As you move forward, keep those empowering beliefs close; let them be your guide through the twists and turns, the crossroads, and the smooth paths. And on the days where that path feels a bit rocky, take a moment, turn around, look back and remind yourself how far you've come. You're not the same person who started this journey, and that's something to celebrate.

You've got everything you need right now within you to do this. I know you can do it if you just follow this process. I believe in you. So, how about you take this new affirmation and repeat it every at every opportunity:

"I believe in me"

Because you deserve it all. This life with new possibilities that feels balanced, harmonious, and happy—you deserve it all, and don't you dare let your mind, or anyone else for that matter, tell you otherwise.

Printed in Great Britain
by Amazon